MW00934330

THIS BOOK BELONGS TO:

_____

_____

_____

COPYRIGHT © 2024 BY GCD PUBLISHING
ALL RIGHTS RESERVED. THIS BOOK OR ANY PORTION THEREOF
MAY NOT BE REPRODUCED OR USED IN ANY MANNER WHATSOEVER
WITHOUT THE EXPRESSED WRITTEN PERMISSION OF THE PUBLISHER.

Are you using markers or pens?

Some coloring materials may bleed through
the paper onto the next page.

Please put a piece of card or paper between
the coloring pages to prevent bleeding to
the next page.

Made in the USA
Monee, IL
15 November 2024

70203404R10044